OAK AND IV

BY

PAUL DUNBAR

DAYTON OHIO
PRESS OF UNITED BRETHREN PUBLISHING HOUSE
1893

TO HER

WHO HAS EVER BEEN

MY GUIDE, TEACHER, AND INSPIRATION,

My Mother,

THIS LITTLE VOLUME IS

Affectionately inscribed.

OAK AND IVY.

Ode to Ethiopia.

O Mother Race! to thee I bring
This pledge of faith unwavering,
  This tribute to thy glory.
I know the pangs which thou didst feel,
When Slavery crushed thee with its heel,
  With thy dear blood all gory.

Sad days were those,—ah, sad indeed!
But through the land the fruitful seed
  Of better times was growing.
The plant of freedom upward sprung,
And spread its leaves so fresh and young,—
  Its blossoms now are blowing.

On every hand in this fair land
Proud Ethiope's swarthy children stand
  Beside their fairer neighbor;
The forests flee before their stroke,
Their hammers ring, their forges smoke,—
  They stir in honest labor.

They tread the fields where honor calls;
Their voices sound through senate halls
  In majesty and power.
To right they cling; the hymns they sing
Up to the skies in beauty ring,
  And bolder grow each hour.

Be proud, my Race, in mind and soul;
Thy name is writ on Glory's scroll
  In characters of fire.
High 'mid the clouds of Fame's bright sky
Thy banner's blazoned folds now fly,
  And truth shall lift them higher.

Thou hast the right to noble pride,
Whose spotless robes were purified
  By blood's severe baptism.
Upon thy brow the cross was laid,
And labor's painful sweat-beads made
  A consecrating chrism.

No other race, or white or black,
When bound, as thou wert, to the rack,
  So seldom stooped to grieving;
No other race, when free again,
Forgot the past and proved them men
  So noble in forgiving.

Go on and up! Our souls and eyes
Shall follow thy continuous rise;
  Our ears shall list thy story
From bards which from thy root shall spring,
And proudly tune their lyres to sing
  Of Ethiopia's glory.

A Drowsy Day.

The air is dark, the sky is gray,
　The misty shadows come and go,
And here within my dusky room
Each chair looks ghostly in the gloom.
　Outside the rain falls cold and slow,—
Half-stinging drops, half-blinding spray.

Each slightest sound is magnified,
　For drowsy quiet holds her reign;
The burnt stick on the fireplace breaks,
The nodding cat with start awakes,
　And then to sleep drops off again,
Unheeding Towser at her side.

I look far out across the lawn,
　Where huddled stand the silly sheep,
My work lies idle at my hands,
My thoughts fly out like scattered strands
　Of thread, and on the verge of sleep—
Still half awake—I dream and yawn.

What spirits rise before my eyes!
　How various of kind and form!
Sweet memories of days long past,
The dreams of youth that could not last,
　Each smiling calm, each raging storm,
That swept across my early skies.

Half seen, the bare, gaunt-fingered boughs
　Before my window sweep and sway,
And chafe in tortures of unrest.
My chin sinks down upon my breast;
　I cannot work on such a day,
But only sit and dream and drowse.

Keep a Pluggin' Away.

I've a humble little motto
That is homely, though it's true,—
  Keep a pluggin' away.
It's a thing when I've an object
That I always try to do,—
  Keep a pluggin' away.
When you've rising storms to quell,
When opposing waters swell,
It will never fail to tell,—
  Keep a pluggin' away.

If the hills are high before
And the paths are hard to climb,
  Keep a pluggin' away.
And remember that success
Comes to him who bides his time,—
  Keep a pluggin' away.
From the greatest to the least,
None are from the rule released.
Be thou toiler, poet, priest,
  Keep a pluggin' away.

Delve away beneath the surface,
There is treasure farther down,—
  Keep a pluggin' away.
Let the rain come down in torrents,
Let the threat'ning heavens frown,
  Keep a pluggin' away.
When the clouds have rolled away,
There will come a brighter day
All your labor to repay,—.
  Keep a pluggin' away.

There'll be lots of sneers to swallow,
There'll be lots of pain to bear,—
   Keep a pluggin' away.
If you've got your eye on heaven,
Some bright day you'll wake up there,—
   Keep a pluggin' away.
Perseverance still is king;
Time its sure reward will bring,
Work and wait unwearying,—
   Keep a pluggin' away.

The Sparrow.

A little bird, with plumage brown,
Beside my window flutters down,
A moment chirps its little strain,
Then taps upon my window pane,
And chirps again, and hops along,
To call my notice to its song;
But I work on, nor heed its lay,
Till, in neglect, it flies away.

So birds of peace and hope and love
Come fluttering earthward from above,
To settle on life's window sills,
And ease our load of earthly ills;
But we, in traffic's rush and din
Too deep engaged to let them in,
With deadened heart and sense plod on,
Nor know our loss till they are gone. ‐

An Easter Ode.

To the cold, dark grave they go
Silently and sad and slow,
From the light of happy skies
And the glance of mortal eyes.
In their beds the violets spring,
And the brook flows murmuring;
But at eve the violets die,
And the brook in the sand runs dry.

In the rosy, blushing morn,
See, the smiling babe is born;
For a day it lives, and then
Breathes its short life out again.
And anon gaunt-visaged Death,
With his keen and icy breath,
Bloweth out the vital fire
In the hoary-headed sire.

Heeding not the children's wail,
Fathers droop and mothers fail;
Sinking sadly from each other,
Sister parts from loving brother.
All the land is filled with wailing,—
Sounds of mourning garments trailing,
With their sad portent imbued,
Making melody subdued.

But in all this depth of woe
This consoling truth we know:
There will come a time of rain,
And the brook will flow again;
Where the violet fell, 'twill grow,
When the sun has chased the snow.
See in this the lesson plain,
Mortal man shall rise again

Well the prophecy was kept;.
Christ—"first fruit of them that slept "—
Rose with vic'try-circled brow;
So, believing one, shalt thou.
Ah! but there shall come a day
When, unhampered by this clay,
Souls shall rise to life newborn
On that resurrection morn.

October.

October is the treasurer of the year,
  And all the months pay bounty to her store;
The fields and orchards still their tribute bear,
  And fill her brimming coffers more and more.
But she, with youthful lavishness,
Spends all her wealth in gaudy dress,
  And decks herself in garments bold
  Of scarlet, purple, red, and gold.

She heedeth not how swift the hours fly,
  But smiles and sings her happy life along;
She only sees above a shining sky;
  She only hears the breezes' voice in song.
Her garments trail the woodlands through,
And gather pearls of early dew
  That sparkle, till the roguish Sun
  Creeps up and steals them every one.

But what cares she that jewels should be lost,
  When all of Nature's bounteous wealth is hers?
Though princely fortunes may have been their cost,
  Not one regret her calm demeanor stirs.
Whole-hearted, happy, careless, free,
She lives her life out joyously,
  Nor cares when Frost stalks o'er her way
  And turns her auburn locks to gray.

Merry Autumn.

It's all a farce,—these tales they tell
   About the breezes sighing,
And moans astir o'er field and dell,
   Because the year is dying.

Such principles are most absurd,—
   I care not who first taught 'em;
There's nothing known to beast or bird
   To make a solemn autumn.

In solemn times, when grief holds sway
   With countenance distressing,
You'll note the more of black and gray
   Will then be used in dressing.

Now purple tints are all around;
   The sky is blue and mellow;
And e'en the grasses turn the ground
   From modest green to yellow.

The seed burs all with laughter crack
   On featherweed and jimson;
And leaves that should be dressed in black
   Are all decked out in crimson.

A butterfly goes winging by;
   A singing bird comes after;
And Nature, all from earth to sky,
   Is bubbling o'er with laughter.

The ripples wimple on the rills,
   Like sparkling little lasses;
The sunlight runs along the hills,
   And laughs among the grasses.

The earth is just so full of fun
　It really can't contain it;
And streams of mirth so freely run
　The heavens seem to rain it.

Don't talk to me of solemn days
　In autumn's time of splendor,
Because the sun shows fewer rays,
　And these grow slant and slender.

Why, it's the climax of the year,—
　The highest time of living!—
Till naturally its bursting cheer
　Just melts into thanksgiving.

Dr. James Newton Matthews, Mason, Ill.

All round about, the clouds encompassed me;
　On every side I looked, my weary sight
　Was met by terrors of Plutonian night;
And chilling surges of a cruel sea
That beat against my stronghold ceaselessly,
　Roared rude derision at my hapless plight,
　And hope, which I had thought to hold so tight,
Slipped from my weak'ning grasp and floated free.

But when I thought to flee the unequal strife,
　As wearied out I could not bear it more,
　Fate gave the choicest gem of all her store,—
And noble Matthews came into my life.
　He warmed my being like a virile flame,
　And with his coming, light and courage came!

A Summer Pastoral.

It's hot to-day. The bees is buzzin'
  Kinder don't-keer-like aroun',
An' fur off the warm air dances
  O'er the parchin' roofs in town.
In the brook the cows is standin';
  Childern hidin' in the hay;
Can't keep none of 'em a workin',
  'Cause it's hot to-day.

It's hot to-day. The sun is blazin'
  Like a great big ball o' fire;
Seems as ef instead o' settin'
  It keeps mountin' higher an' higher.
I'm as triflin' as the childern,
- Though I blame them lots an' scold;
I keep slippin' to the spring house,
  Where the milk is rich an' cold.

The very air within its shadder
  Smells o' cool an' restful things,
An' a roguish little robin
  Sits above the place an' sings.
I don't mean to be a shirkin',
  But I linger by the way
Longer, mebbe, than is needful,
  'Cause it's hot to-day.

It's hot to-day. The horses stumble
  Half asleep across the fiel's;
An' a host o' teasin' fancies
  O'er my burnin' senses steals,—
Dreams o' cool rooms, curtains lowered,
  An' a sofy's temptin' look;
Patter o' composin' raindrops
  Or the ripple of a brook.

I strike a stump! That wakes me sudden;
  Dreams all vanish into air.
Lordy! how I chew my whiskers;
  'Twouldn't do fur me to swear.
But I have to be so keerful
  'Bout my thoughts an' what I say;
Somethin' might slip out unheeded,
  'Cause it's hot to-day.

Git up, there, Suke! you, Sal, git over!
  Sakes alive! how I do sweat.
Every stitch that I've got on me,
  Bet a cent, is wringin' wet.
If this keeps up, I'll lose my temper.
  Gee there, Sal, you lazy brute!
Wonder who on airth this weather
  Could 'a' be'n got up to suit?

You, Sam, go bring a tin o' water;
  Dash it all, don't be so slow!
'Pears as ef you tuk an hour
  'Tween each step to stop an' blow.
Think I want to stand a meltin'
  Out here in this 'b'ilin' sun,
While you stop to think about it?
  Lift them feet o' your'n an' run.

It ain't no use; I'm plumb fetaggled.
  Come an' put this team away.
I won't plow another furrer;
  It's too mortal hot to-day.
I ain't weak, nor I ain't lazy,
  But I'll stand this half day's loss
'Fore I let the devil make me
  Lose my patience an' git cross.

Songs.

A bee that was searching for sweets one day
Through the gate of a rose garden happened to stray.
In the heart of a rose he hid away,
And forgot in his bliss the light of day,
As sipping his honey he buzzed in song;
Though day was waning, he lingered long,
    For the rose was sweet, so sweet.

A robin sits pluming his ruddy breast,
And a madrigal sings to his love in her nest:
"Oh, the skies they are blue, the fields are green,
And the birds in your nest will soon be seen!"
She hangs on his words with a thrill of love,
And chirps to him as he sits above,
    For the song is sweet, so sweet.

A maiden was out on a summer's day
With the winds and the waves and the flowers at play;
And she met with a youth of gentle air,
With the light of the sunshine on his hair.
Together they wandered the flowers among;
They loved, and loving they lingered long,
    For to love is sweet, so sweet.

———

Bird of my lady's bow'r,
  Sing her a song;
Tell her that ev'ry hour,
  All the day long,
Thoughts of her come to me,
  Filling my brain
With the warm ecstasy
  Of love's refrain.

Little bird! happy bird!
  Being so near,
Where e'en her slightest word
  Thou mayest hear,
Seeing her glancing eyes,
  Sheen of her hair,
Thou art in paradise,—
  Would I were there.

I am so far away,
  Thou art so near;
Plead with her, birdling gay,
  Plead with my dear.
Rich be thy recompense,
  Fine be thy fee,
If through thine eloquence
  She hearken me.

Sunset.

The river sleeps beneath the sky,
  And clasps the shadows to its breast;
The crescent moon shines dim on high;
  And in the lately radiant west
    The gold is fading into gray.
    Now stills the lark his festive lay
    And mourns with me the dying day,—

While in the south the first faint star
  Lifts to the night its silver face,
And twinkles to the moon afar
  Across the heaven's graying space;
    Low murmurs reach me from the town,
    As Day puts on her somber crown,
    And shakes her mantle darkly down.

In Summer Time.

When summer time has come, and all
The world is in the magic thrall
Of perfumed airs that lull each sense
To fits of drowsy indolence;
When skies are deepest blue above,
And flow'rs aflush,—then most I love
To start, while early dews are damp,
And wend my way in woodland tramp
Where forests rustle, tree on tree,
And sing their silent songs to me;
Where pathways meet and pathways part,—
To walk with Nature heart by heart,
Till wearied out at last I lie
Where some sweet stream steals singing by
A mossy bank; where violets vie
In color with the summer sky,—
Or take my rod and line and hook,
And wander to some darkling brook,
Where all day long the willows dream,
And idly droop to kiss the stream,
And there to loll from morn till night—
Unheeding nibble, run, or bite—
Just for the joy of being there
And drinking in the summer air,
The summer sounds, and summer sights,
That set a restless mind to rights ·
When grief and pain and raging doubt
Of men and creeds have worn it out;
The birds' song and the water's drone,
The humming bees' low monotone,
The murmur of the passing breeze,
And all the sounds akin to these,
That make a man in summer time
Feel only fit for rest and rhyme.

Joy springs all radiant in my breast;
Though pauper poor, than king more blest,
The tide beats in my soul so strong
That happiness breaks forth in song,
And rings aloud the welkin blue
With all the songs I ever knew.
O time of rapture! time of song!
How swiftly glide thy days along
Adown the current of the years,
Above the rocks of grief and tears!
'Tis wealth enough of joy for me
In summer time to simply be.

Hymn.

When storms arise
And darkening skies
About me threat'ning lower,
  To thee, O Lord, I lift mine eyes,
  To thee my tortured spirit flies
For solace in that hour.

Thy mighty arm
Will let no harm
Come near me nor befall me.
  Thy voice shall quiet my alarm,
  When life's great battle waxeth warm,
No foeman shall appall me.

Upon thy breast
Secure I rest
From sorrow and vexation,
  No more by sinful cares oppressed,
  But in thy presence ever blest,
O God of my salvation!

A Banjo Song.

Oh, dere's lots o' care an' trouble
  In dis world to swaller down;
An' ol' Sorrer's purty lively
  In her way o' gittin' roun'.
Yet dere's times when I furgit 'em,—
  Aches an' pains an' troubles all,—
An' it's when I take at ebenin'
  My ol' banjo f'um de wall.

'Bout de time dat night is fallin'
  An' my daily wu'k is done,
An' above de shady hilltops
  I kin see de settin' sun;
When de quiet, restful shadders
  Is beginnin' jes' to fall,—
Den I take de little banjo
  F'um its place upon de wall.

Den my fam'ly gadders roun' me
  In de fadin' o' de light,
As I strike de strings to try 'em
  Ef dey all is tuned cr-right.
An' it seems we're so nigh heaben
  We kin hyeah de angels sing
When de music o' dat banjo
  Sets my cabin all er-ring.

An' my wife an' all de chillen,—
  Male an' female, small an' big,—
Even up to gray-haired granny,
  Seem jes' boun' to do a jig;
Till I change de style o' music,
  Change de movement an' de time,
An' de ringin' little banjo
  Plays an ol' heart-feelin' hime.

An' somehow my th'oat gits choky,
  An' a lump keeps tryin' to rise,
Like it wan'ed to ketch de water
  Dat was flowin' to my eyes;
An' I feel dat I could sorter
  Knock de socks clean off o' sin
As I hyeah my po' ol' granny
  Wid her tremblin' voice jine in.

Den we all th'ow in our voices
  Fur to he'p de chune out too,
Like a big camp-meetin' choiry
  Tryin' to sing a mou'nah th'oo.
An' our th'oats let out de music,
  Sweet an' solemn, loud an' free,
Till de rafters o' my cabin
  Echo wid de melody.

Oh, de music o' de banjo,
  Quick an' deb'lish, solemn, slow,
Is de greates' joy an' solace
  Dat a weary slave kin know!
So jes' let me hyeah it ringin',
  Do' de chune be po' an' rough,
It's a pleasure; an' de pleasures
  O' dis life is few enough.

Now, de blessed little angels
  Up in heaben, we are told,
Don't do nothin' all dere lifetime
  'Ceptin' play on ha'ps o' gold.
Now I think heaben'd be mo' homelike
  Ef we'd hyeah some music fall
F'um a real ol'-fashioned banjo,
  Like dat one upon de wall.

The Ol' Tunes.

You kin talk about yer anthems
    An' yer arias an' sich,
An' yer modern choir singin'
    That you think so awful rich;
But you orter heerd us youngsters
    In the times now far away,
A singin' o' the ol' tunes
    In the ol'-fashioned way.

There was some o' us sung treble,
    An' a few o' us growled bass,
An' the tide o' song flowed smoothly
    With its complement o' grace;
There was spirit in that music,
    An' a kind o' solemn sway,
A singin' o' the old tunes
    In the ol'-fashioned way.

I remember oft o' standin'
    In my homespun pantaloons,—
On my face the bronze an' freckles
    O' the suns o' youthful Junes,—
Thinkin' that no mortal minstrel
    Ever chanted sich a lay
As the ol' tunes we was singin'
    In the ol'-fashioned way.

The boys 'ud always lead us,
    An' the girls 'ud all chime in,
Till the sweetness o' the singin'
    Robbed the list'nin' soul o' sin;
An' I ust to tell the parson
    'Twas as good to sing as pray,
When the people sung the ol' tunes
    In the ol'-fashioned way.

How I long agin to hear it,
　Pourin' forth from soul to soul,
With the treble high an' meller,
　An' the bass's mighty roll;
But the times is very diff'rent,
　An' the music heerd to-day
Ain't the singin' o' the ol' tunes
　In the ol'-fashioned way.

Little screechin' by a woman,
　Little squawkin' by a man,
Then the organ's twiddle-twaddle,
　Jest the empty space to span,—
An' ef you should even think it,
　'Tisn't proper fur to say
That you want to hear the ol' tunes
　In the ol'-fashioned way.

But I think that some bright mornin',
　When the toils of life is o'er,
An' the sun o' heaven arisin'
　Glads with light the happy shore,
I shall hear the angel chorus,
　In the realms o' endless day,
A singin' o' the ol' tunes
　In the ol'-fashioned way.

Lullaby.

Sing me, sweet, a soothing psalm,
Holy, tender, low, and calm,
Full of drowsy words and dreamy,
Sleep half seen where the sides are seamy;
Lay my head upon your breast;
　　　　Sing me to rest

Christmas Carol.

Ring out, ye bells!
All Nature swells
With gladness at the wondrous story,—
The world was lorn,
But Christ is born
To change our sadness into glory.

Sing, earthlings, sing!
To-night a King
Hath come from heaven's high throne to bless us.
The outstretched hand
O'er all the land
Is raised in pity to caress us

Come at his call;
Be joyful all;
Away with mourning and with sadness!
The heavenly choir
With holy fire
Their voices raise in songs of gladness.

The darkness breaks,
And Dawn awakes,
Her cheeks suffused with youthful blushes.
The rocks and stones
In holy tones
Are singing sweeter than the thrushes.

Then why should we
In silence be,
When Nature lends her voice to praises;
When heaven and earth
Proclaim the truth
Of Him for whom that lone star blazes?

No, be not still,
But with a will
Strike all your harps and set them ringing;
On hill and heath
Let every breath
Throw all its power into singing!

Welcome Address

TO THE WESTERN ASSOCIATION OF WRITERS.

"Westward the course of empire takes its way,"—
So Berkeley said, and so to-day
The men who know the world still say.
The glowing West, with bounteous hand,
Bestows her gifts throughout the land,
And smiles to see at her command
Art, science, and the industries,—
New fruits of new Hesperides.
So, proud are you who claim the West
As home land; doubly are you blest
To live where liberty and health
Go hand in hand with brains and wealth.
So here's a welcome to you all,
Whate'er the work your hands let fall,—
To you who trace on history's page
The footprints of each passing age;
To you who tune the laureled lyre
To songs of love or deeds of fire;
To you before whose well-wrought tale
The cheek doth flush or brow grow pale;
To you who bow the ready knee
And worship cold philosophy,—
A welcome warm as Western wine,
And free as Western hearts, be thine.
Do what the greatest joy insures,—
The city has no will but yours!

JUNE 27, 1892.

𝕿𝖍𝖊 𝕺𝖑𝖉 𝕬𝖕𝖕𝖑𝖊 𝕿𝖗𝖊𝖊.

There's a memory keeps a runnin'
    Through my weary head to-night,
An' I see a picture dancin'
    In the fire flames' ruddy light;
'Tis the picture of an orchard
    Wrapped in autumn's purple haze,
With the tender light about it
    That I loved in other days.
An' a standin' in a corner
    Once again I seem to see
The verdant leaves an' branches
    Of an old apple tree.

You perhaps would call it ugly,
    An' I don't know but it's so,
When you look the tree all over
    Unadorned by memory's glow;
For its boughs are gnarled an' crooked,
    An' its leaves are gettin' thin,
An' the apples of its bearin'
    Wouldn't fill so large a bin
As they ust to. But I tell you,
    When it comes to pleasin' me,
It's the dearest in the orchard,—
    Is that old apple tree.

I would hide within its shelter,
    Settlin' in some cozy nook,
Where no calls nor threats could stir me
    From the pages o' my book.
Oh, that quiet, sweet seclusion
    In its fullness passeth words!
It was deeper than the deepest
    That my sanctum now affords.
Why, the jaybirds an' the robins,
    They was hand in glove with me,
As they winked at me an' warbled
    In that old apple tree.

It was on its sturdy branches
  That in summers long ago
I would tie my swing, an' dangle
  In contentment to an' fro,
Idly dreamin' childish fancies,
  Buildin' castles in the air,
Makin' o' myself a hero
  Of romances rich an' rare.
I kin shet my eyes an' see it
  Jest as plain as plain kin be,
That same old swing a danglin'
  To the old apple tree.

There's a rustic seat beneath it
  That I never kin forget.
It's the place where me an' Hallie—
  Little sweetheart—ust to set,
When we'd wander to the orchard
  So's no listenin' ones could hear
As I whispered sugared nonsense
  Into her little willin' ear.
Now my gray old wife is Hallie,
  An' I'm grayer still than she,
But I'll not forget our courtin'
  'Neath the old apple tree.

Life for us ain't all been summer,
  But I guess we've had our share
Of its flittin' joys an' pleasures,
  An' a sprinklin' of its care.
Oft the skies have smiled upon us;
  Then again we've seen 'em frown,
Though our load was ne'er so heavy
  That we longed to lay it down.
But when death does come a callin',
  This my last request shall be,—
That they'll bury me an' Hallie
  'Neath the old apple tree

James Whitcomb Riley.

FROM A WESTERNER'S POINT OF VIEW.

No matter what you call it,
  Whether genius, gift, or art,
He sings the simple songs that come
  The closest to your heart.
Fur trim an' skillful phrases,
  I do not keer a jot;
'Tain't the words alone, but feelin's,
  That tech the tender spot.
An' that's jest why I love him,—
  Why, he's got sech human feelin',
An' in ev'ry song he gives us,
  You kin see it creepin', stealin'.
Through the core the tears go tricklin',
  But the edge is bright an' smiley;
I never saw a poet
  Like that poet Whitcomb Riley.

His heart keeps beatin' time with our'n
  In measures fast or slow;
He tells us jest the same ol' things
  Our souls have learned to know.
He paints our joys an' sorrers
  In a way so stric'ly true,
That a body can't help knowin'
  That he has felt them too.
If there's a lesson to be taught,
  He never fears to teach it,
An' he puts the food so good an' low
  That the humblest one kin reach it.
Now in our time, when poets rhyme
  For money, fun, or fashion,
'Tis good to hear one voice so clear
  That thrills with honest passion.
So let the others build their songs,
  An' strive to polish highly,—
There's none of them kin tech the heart
  Like our own Whitcomb Riley.

A Thanksgiving Poem.

The sun hath shed its kindly light,
  Our harvesting is gladly o'er,
Our fields have felt no killing blight,
  Our bins are filled with goodly store.

From pestilence, fire, flood, and sword
  We have been spared by thy decree,
And now with humble hearts, O Lord,
  We come to pay our thanks to thee.

We feel that had our merits been
  The measure of thy gifts to us,
We erring children, born of sin,
  Might not now be rejoicing thus.

No deed of ours hath brought us grace;
  When thou wert nigh our sight was dull,
We hid in trembling from thy face,
  But thou, O God, wert merciful.

Thy mighty hand o'er all the land
  Hath still been open to bestow
Those blessings which our wants demand
  From heaven, whence all blessings flow.

Thou hast, with ever watchful eye,
  Looked down on us with holy care,
And from thy storehouse in the sky
  Hast scattered plenty everywhere.

Then lift we up our songs of praise
  To thee, O Father, good and kind;
To thee we consecrate our days;
  Be thine the temple of each mind.

With incense sweet our thanks ascend,
  Before thy works our powers pall;
Though we should strive years without end,
  We could not thank thee for them all.

To Miss Mary Britton.

When the legislature of Kentucky was discussing the passage of a separate-coach bill, Miss Mary Britton, a teacher in the schools of Lexington, Kentucky, went before them, and in a ringing speech protested against the passage of the bill. Her action was heroic, though it proved to be without avail.

God of the right, arise
  And let thy pow'r prevail;
Too long thy children mourn
  In labor and travail.
Oh, speed the happy day
  When waiting ones may see
The glory-bringing birth
  Of our real liberty!

Grant thou, O gracious God,
  That not in word alone
Shall freedom's boon be ours,
  While bondage-galled we moan!
But condescend to us
  In our o'erwhelming need;
Break down the hind'ring bars,
  And make us free indeed.

Give us to lead our cause
  More noble souls like hers,
The memory of whose deed
  Each feeling bosom stirs;
Whose fearless voice and strong
  Rose to defend her race,
Roused Justice from her sleep,
  Drove Prejudice from place.

Let not the mellow light
  Of Learning's brilliant ray
Be quenched, to turn to night
  Our newly dawning day.

To that bright, shining star
  Which thou didst set in place,
With universal voice
  Thus speaks a grateful race:

"Not empty words shall be
  Our offering to your fame;
The race you strove to serve
  Shall consecrate your name.
Speak on as fearless still;
  Work on as tireless ever;
And your reward shall be
  Due meed for your endeavor."

Whittier.

Not o'er thy dust let there be spent
The gush of maudlin sentiment;
Such drift as that is not for thee,
Whose life and deeds and songs agree,
Sublime in their simplicity.

Nor shall the sorrowing tear be shed;
O singer sweet, thou art not dead!
In spite of time's malignant chill,
With living fire thy songs shall thrill,
And men shall say, "He liveth still!"

Great poets never die, for Earth
Doth count their lives of too great worth
To lose them from her treasured store;
So shalt thou live for evermore—
Though far thy form from mortal ken—
Deep in the hearts and minds of men.

Nutting Song.

The November sun invites me,
And although the chill wind smites me,
I will wander to the woodland
    Where the laden trees await;
And with loud and joyful singing
I will set the forest ringing,
As if I were king of Autumn,
    And Dame Nature were my mate,—

While the squirrel in his gambols
Fearless round about me ambles,
As if he were bent on showing
    In my kingdom he'd a share;
While my warm blood leaps and dashes,
And my eye with freedom flashes,
As my soul drinks deep and deeper
    Of the magic in the air.

There's a pleasure found in nutting,
All life's cares and griefs outshutting,
That is fuller far and better
    Than what prouder sports impart.
Who could help a carol trilling
As he sees the baskets filling?
Why, the flow of song keeps running
    O'er the high walls of the heart.

So when I am home returning,
When the sun is lowly burning,
I will once more wake the echoes
    With a happy song of praise,—
For the golden sunlight blessing,
And the breezes' soft caressing,
And the precious boon of living
    In the sweet November days.

After While.

A POEM OF FAITH.

I think that though the clouds be dark,
That though the waves dash o'er the bark,
Yet after while the light will come,
And in calm waters safe at home
    The bark will anchor.
Weep not, my sad-eyed, gray-robed maid,
Because your fairest blossoms fade,
That sorrow still o'erruns your cup,
And even though you root them up,
    The weeds grow ranker.

For after while your tears shall cease,
And sorrow shall give way to peace;
The flow'rs shall bloom, the weeds shall die,
And in that faith seen, by and by
    Thy woes shall perish.
Smile at old Fortune's adverse tide,
Smile when the scoffers sneer and chide.
Oh, not for you the gems that pale,
And not for you the flow'rs that fail;
    Let this thought cherish:

That after while the clouds will part,
And then with joy the waiting heart
Shall feel the light come stealing in,
That drives away the cloud of sin
    And breaks its power.
And you shall burst your chrysalis,
And wing away to realms of bliss,
Untrammeled, pure, divinely free,
Above all earth's anxiety
    From that same hour.

To the Miami.

Kiss me, Miami, thou most constant one!
   I love thee more for that thou changest not.
When Winter comes with frigid blast,
Or when the blithesome Spring is past
   And Summer's here with sunshine hot,
Or in sere Autumn, thou hast still the pow'r
To charm alike, whate'er the hour.

Kiss me, Miami, with thy dewy lips;
   Throbs fast my heart e'en as thine own breast beats.
My soul doth rise as rise thy waves,
As each on each the dark shore laves
   And breaks in ripples and retreats.
There is a poem in thine every phase;
Thou still has sung through all thy days.

Tell me, Miami, how it was with thee
   When years ago Tecumseh in his prime
His birch boat o'er thy waters sent,
And pitched upon thy banks his tent.
   In that long-gone, poetic time,
Did some bronze bard thy flowing stream sit by
And sing thy praises, e'en as I?

Did some bronze lover 'neath this dark old tree
   Whisper of love unto his Indian maid?
And didst thou list his murmurs deep,
And in thy bosom safely keep
   The many raging vows they said?
Or didst thou tell to fish and frog and bird
The raptured scenes that there occurred?

But, O dear stream, what volumes thou couldst tell
   To all who know thy language as I do,
Of life and love and jealous hate!
But now to tattle were too late,—
   Thou who hast ever been so true.
Tell not to every passing idler here
All those sweet tales that reached thine ear.

But, silent stream, speak out and tell me this:
  I say that men and things are still the same;
Were men as bold to do and dare?
Were women then as true and fair?
  Did poets seek celestial flame,
The hero die to gain a laureled brow,
And women suffer, then as now?

Love's Pictures.

Like the blush upon the rose
  When the wooing south wind speaks,
Kissing soft its petals,
  Are thy cheeks.

Tender, soft, beseeching, true,
  Like the stars that deck the skies
Through the ether sparkling,
  Are thine eyes.

Like the song of happy birds,
  When the woods with spring rejoice,
In their blithe awak'ning,
  Is thy voice.

Like soft threads of clustered silk
  O'er thy face so pure and fair,
Sweet in its profusion,
  Is thy hair.

Like a fair but fragile vase,
  Triumph of the carver's art,
Graceful formed and slender,—
  Thus thou art.

Ah, thy cheek, thine eyes, thy voice,
  And thy hair's delightful wave
Make me, I'll confess it,
  Thy poor slave!

The "Chronic Kicker."

It was at the town convention
  Fur to nominate a mayor,
An' things had been progressin'
  In a way both cool an' fair;
An' we thought that we had finished
  In a manner mighty slick,
When up rose the chronic kicker
  Fur to kick, kick, kick.

Then we felt our feathers fallin',
  Nor we didn't laugh no more,
While some quite impatient fellers
  Made a bee line fur the door,
An' we listened, an' we listened,
  While the clock the hours ticked,
To that derned old chronic kicker
  As he kicked, kicked, kicked.

Next we held a conf'rence meetin'
  In our little mission church,—
Fur a cheap an' worthy pastor
  We were in an earnest search;
We had jest made our agreement
  (An' 'twas come to very quick),
When up rose the chronic kicker
  Fur to kick, kick, kick.

An' we heard the birds a whistlin'
  In the air so sweet an' cool,
While we all sat there a list'nin'
  To that flambergasted fool;
But I'm sure the Lord was min'ful,
  Fur no thorn our conscience pricked,
When we nodded while that kicker
  Stood an' kicked, kicked, kicked.

Next 'twas in a baseball battle,
  Overlooked by boys in trees,
Where no act of bat or baseman
  Could this chronic kicker please,
Until weary with his yellin',
  Some one hit him with a brick,
An' he lay down in the diamond
  Fur to kick, kick, kick.

But Death, that great policeman,
  By no frowns or kicks defied,
At last came up an' seized him,
  An' so, with a kick, he died;
But he, jest before the fun'ral,
  Made the undertaker sick,
As the coffin couldn't hold him
  For that everlastin' kick.

Songs.

I love the dear old ballads best,
  That tell of love and death,
Whose every line sings love's unrest
  Or mourns the parting breath.
I love those songs the heart can feel,
  That make our pulses throb;
When lovers plead or contrites kneel
  With choking sigh and sob.

God sings through songs that touch the heart,
  And none are prized save these.
Though men may ply their gilded art
  For fortune, fame, or fees,
The muse that sets the songster's soul
  Ablaze with lyric fire,
Holds nature up, an open scroll,
  And builds art's funeral pyre.

My Sort o' Man.

I don't believe in 'ristercrats
    An' never did, you see;
The plain ol' homelike sorter folks
    Is good enough fur me.
O' course, I don't desire a man
    To be too tarnal rough,
But then I think all folks should know
    When they air nice enough.

Now, there is folks in this here world,
    From peasant up to king,
Who want to be so awful nice
    They overdo the thing.
That's jest the thing that makes me sick,
    An' quicker than a wink
I set it down that them same folks
    Ain't half so good's you think.

I like to see a man dress nice,
    In clothes becomin', too;
I like to see a woman fix
    As women orter do;
An' boys an' gals' I like to see
    Look fresh an' young an' spry,—
We all must have our vanity
    An' pride before we die.

But I jedge no man by his clothes,—
    Nor gentleman nor tramp;
The man that wears the finest suit
    May be the biggest scamp,
An' he whose limbs are clad in rags
    That make a mournful sight,
In life's great battle may have proved
    A hero in the fight.

I don't believe in 'ristercrats;
  I like the honest tan
That lies upon the healthful cheek
  An' speaks the honest man;
I like to grasp the brawny hand
  That labor's lips have kissed,
For he who has not labored here
  Life's greatest pride has missed,—

The pride to feel that yo'r own strength
  Has cleaved fur you the way
To heights to which you were not born,
  But struggled day by day.
What though the thousands sneer an' scoff,
  An' scorn yo'r humble birth?
Kings are but subjects; you are king
  By right o' royal worth.

The man who simply sits an' waits
  Fur good to come along,
Ain't worth the breath that one would take
  To tell him he is wrong.
Fur good ain't flowin' round this world
  Fur ev'ry fool to sup;
You've got to put yo'r see-ers on,
  An' go an' hunt it up.

Good goes with honesty, I say,
  To honor an' to bless;
To rich an' poor alike it brings
  A wealth o' happiness.
The 'ristercrats ain't got it all,
  Fur much to their su'prise,
That's one of earth's most blessed things
  They can't monopolize.

The Old Homestead.

'Tis an old deserted homestead
  On the outskirts of the town,
Where the roof is all moss-covered,
  And the walls are tumbling down;
But around that little cottage
  Do my brightest mem'ries cling,
For 'twas there I spent the moments
  Of my youth,—life's happy spring.

I remember how I used to
  Swing upon the old front gate,
While the robin in the tree tops
  Sung a night song to his mate;
And how later in the evening,
  As the beaux were wont to do,
Mr. Perkins, in the parlor,
  Sat and sparked my sister Sue.

There my mother—heaven bless her!—
  Kissed or spanked as was our need,
And by smile or stroke implanted
  In our hearts fair virtue's seed;
While my father, man of wisdom,
  Lawyer keen, and farmer stout,
Argued long with neighbor Dobbins
  How the corn crops would turn out.

Then the quiltings and the dances—
  How my feet were wont to fly,
While the moon peeped through the barn chinks
  From her stately place on high.
Oh, those days, so sweet, so happy,
  Ever backward o'er me roll;
Still the music of that farm life
  Rings an echo in my soul.

Now the old place is deserted,
　And the walls are falling down;
All who made the home life cheerful,
　Now have died or moved to town.
But about that dear old cottage
　Shall my mem'ries ever cling,
For 'twas there I spent the moments
　Of my youth,—life's happy spring.

On the Death of W. C.

Thou arrant robber, Death!
Couldst thou not find
Some lesser one than he
To rob of breath,—
Some poorer mind
Thy prey to be?

His mind was like the sky,—
　As pure and free;
His heart was broad and open
　As the sea.
His soul shone purely through his face,
And Love made him her dwelling place.

Not less the scholar than the friend, ,
　Not less a friend than man;
The manly life did shorter end
　Because so broad it ran.

Weep not for him, unhappy Muse!
His merits found a grander use
Some other-where.　God wisely sees
The place that needs his qualities.
Weep not for him, for when Death lowers
O'er youth's ambrosia-scented bowers
He only plucks the choicest flowers.

An Old Memory.

How sweet the music sounded
  That summer long ago,
When you were by my side, love,
  To list its gentle flow

I saw your eyes ashining,
  I felt your rippling hair,
I kissed your pearly cheek, love,
  And had no thought of care.

And gay or sad the music,
  With subtle charm replete;
I found in after years, love,
  'Twas you that made it sweet.

For standing where we heard it,
  I hear again the strain;
It wakes my heart, but thrills it
  With sad, mysterious pain.

It pulses not so joyous
  As when you stood with me,
And hand in hand we listened
  To that low melody.

Oh, could the years turn back, love!
  Oh, could events be changed
To what they were that time, love,
  Before we were estranged;

Wert thou once more a maiden
  Whose smile was gold to me;
Were I once more the lover
  Whose word was life to thee,—

O God! could all be altered,
  The pain, the grief, the strife,
And wert thou—as thou shouldst be—
  My true and loyal wife!

But all my tears are idle,
  And all my wishes vain.
What once you were to me, love,
  You may not be again.

For I, alas! like others,
  Have missed my dearest aim.
I asked for love. Oh, mockery!
  Fate comes to me with fame!

Memorial Day.

Why deck with flow'rs these humble mounds?
  Why gather round this fast decaying mold?
Why doth remembrance keep her solemn rounds
  And wrap these sleepers in her loving fold?
    Why kneel, ye silent mourners, here
    To drop the reverential tear?
Flesh is but dust when parted from the breath.

Flesh is but dust, but worth of soul is gold!
  'Tis not the dust we 'honor, but the brave
And noble spirits that it once did hold.
  So kneel we weeping at the grave,
    As at the door through which have passed,
    To enter into mansions vast,
The heroes who have gone to meet
A dearer destiny than dirgeful death.

Melancholia.

Silently without my window,
  Tapping gently at the pane,
  Falls the rain.
Through the trees sighs the breeze
  Like a soul in pain.
Here alone I sit and weep;
Thought hath banished sleep.

Wearily I sit and listen
  To the water's ceaseless drip.
  To my lip
Fate turns up the bitter cup,
  Forcing me to sip;
'Tis a bitter, bitter drink.
Thus I sit and think,—

Thinking things unknown and awful,
  Thoughts on wild, uncanny themes,
  Waking dreams.
Specters dark, corpses stark,
  Show the gaping seams
Whence the cold and cruel knife
Stole away their life.

Bloodshot eyes all strained and staring,
  Gazing ghastly into mine;
  Blood like wine
On the brow—clotted now—
  Shows death's dreadful sign.
Lonely vigil still I keep;
Would that I might sleep!

Still, oh, still, my brain is whirling!
  Still runs on my stream of thought;
  I am caught
In the net fate hath set.
  Mind and soul are brought
To destruction's very brink;
Yet I can but think!

Eyes that look into the future,—
  Peeping forth from out my mind,
  They will find
Some new weight, soon or late,
  On my soul to bind,
Crushing all its courage out,—
Heavier than doubt.

Dawn, the Eastern monarch's daughter,
  Rising from her dewy bed,
  Lays her head
'Gainst the clouds' somber shrouds
  Now half fringed with red.
O'er the land she 'gins to peep;
Come, O gentle Sleep!

Hark! the morning cock is crowing;
  Dreams, like ghosts, must hie away;
  'Tis the day.
Rosy morn now is born;
  Dark thoughts may not stay.
Day my brain from foes will keep;
Now, my soul, I sleep.

Life.

A crust of bread and a corner to sleep in,
A minute to smile and an hour to weep in,
A pint of joy to a peck of trouble,
And never a laugh but the moans come double;
  And that is life!

A crust and a corner that love makes precious,
With the smile to warm and the tears to refresh us;
And joy seems sweeter when cares come after,
And a moan is the finest of foils for laughter;
  And that is life!

A Question.

I wist not that I had the pow'r to sing,
  But here of late they say my songs are sweet.
Is it because my timid numbers ring
  With love's warm music that doth ever beat
Its melody within my throbbing heart?
  If so, what else can roguish Cupid do?
I know him master of the archer's art;
  Is he a trained musician too?

Worn Out.

You bid me hold my peace
  And dry my fruitless tears,
Forgetting that I bear
  A pain beyond my years.

You say that I should smile
  And drive the gloom away;
I would, but sun and smiles
  Have left my life's dark day.

All time seems cold and void,
  And naught but tears remain;
Life's music beats for me
  A melancholy strain.

I used at first to hope,
  But hope is past and gone;
And now without a ray
  My cheerless life drags on.

Like to an ash-stained hearth
  When all its fires are spent;
Like to an autumn wood
  By storm winds rudely shent,—

So sadly goes my heart,
  Unclothed of hope and peace;
It asks not joy again,
  But only seeks release.

A Career.

" Break me my bounds, and let me fly
To regions vast of boundless sky;
Nor I, like piteous Daphne, be
Root-bound. Ah, no! I would be free
As yon same bird that in its flight
Outstrips the range of mortal sight;
Free as the mountain streams that gush
From bubbling springs, and downward rush
Across the serrate mountain's side,—
The rocks o'erwhelmed, their banks defied,—
And like the passions in the soul,
Swell into torrents as they roll.
Oh, circumscribe me not by rules
That serve to lead the minds of fools!
But give me pow'r to work my will,
And at my deeds the world shall thrill.
My words shall rouse the slumb'ring zest
That hardly stirs in manhood's breast;
And as the sun feeds lesser lights,
As planets have their satellites,
So round about me will I bind
The men who prize a master mind!"

        *   *   *   *   *   *

He lived a silent life alone,
And laid him down when it was done;
And at his head was placed a stone
On which was carved a name unknown!

On the River.

The sun is low,
The waters flow,
My boat is dancing to and fro.
The eve is still,
Yet from the hill
The killdeer echoes loud and shrill.

The paddles plash,
The wavelets dash,
We see the summer lightning flash;
While now and then,
In marsh and fen
Too muddy for the feet of men,

Where neither bird
Nor beast has stirred,
The spotted bullfrog's croak is heard.
The wind is high,
The grasses sigh,
The sluggish stream goes sobbing by.

And far away
The dying day
Has cast its last effulgent ray,
While on the land
The shadows stand
Proclaiming that the eve's at hand.

The Light.

Once when my soul was newly shriven,
When perfect peace to me was given,
Pervading all in all with currents bright,
I saw shine forth a mighty Light;
And myriad lesser lights to this were joined,
Each light with every other light entwined;

And as they shone a sound assailed my ears,
Alike the mighty music of the spheres.
The greater light was Love and Peace and Law,
And it had power toward it the rest to draw;
It was the Soul of souls, the greatest One,
The Life of lives, of suns the Sun.
And floating through it all, my soul could see
The Christ-light, shining for humanity;
And silently I heard soft murmurs fall,
"Look up, earth child; the light is all."

John Boyle O'Reilly.

Of noble minds and noble hearts
　　Old Ireland has goodly store;
But thou wert still the noblest son
　　That e'er the Isle of Erin bore.
A generous race, and strong to dare,
　　With hearts as true as purest gold,
With hands to soothe as well as strike,
　　As generous as they are bold,—
This is the race thou lovedst so;
　　And knowing them, I can but know
The glory thy whole being felt
　　To think, to act, to be, the Celt!

Not Celt alone, America
　　Her arms about thee hath entwined;
The noblest traits of each grand race
　　In thee were happily combined
As sweet of song as strong of speech,
　　Thy great heart beat in every line.
No narrow partisan wert thou;
　　The cause of all oppressed was thine!
The world is cruel still and cold,
But who can doubt thy life has told?
Though wrong and sorrow still are rife
Old Earth is better for thy life!

4

OAK AND IVY.

Columbian Ode.

I

Four hundred years ago a tangled waste
  Lay sleeping on the west Atlantic side;
Their devious ways the Old World's millions traced
  Content, and loved and labored, dared and died,
While students still believed the charts they conned,
  And wallowed in their thriftless ignorance,
Nor dreamed of other lands that lay beyond
  Old Ocean's dense, indefinite expanse.

II

But deep within her heart old Nature knew
  That she had once arrayed, at Earth's behest,
Another offspring, fine and fair to view,—
  The chosen suckling of the mother's breast.
The child was wrapped in vestments soft and fine,
  Each fold a work of Nature's matchless art;
The mother looked on it with love divine,
  And strained the loved one closely to her heart.
And there it lay, and with the warmth grew strong
  And hearty, by the salt sea breezes fanned,
Till Time with mellowing touches passed along,
  And changed the infant to a mighty land.

III

But men knew naught of this, till there arose
  That mighty mariner, the Genoese,
Who dared to try, in spite of fears and foes,
  The unknown fortunes of unsounded seas.
O noblest of Italia's sons, thy bark
  Went not alone into that shrouding night.
O dauntless darer of the rayless dark,
  The world sailed with thee to eternal light.

The deer haunts that with game were crowded then
   To-day are tilled and cultivated lands;
The schoolhouse tow'rs where bruin had his den,
   And where the wigwam stood the chapel stands;
The place that nurtured men of savage mien
   Now teems with men of Nature's noblest types;
Where moved the forest-foliage banner green,
   Now flutters in the breeze the stars and stripes!

OCTOBER 21, 1892.

The Meadow Lark.

Though the winds be dank,
  And the sky be sober,
    And the grieving day
    In a mantle gray
Hath let her waiting maiden robe her,—
    All the fields along
    I can hear the song
Of the meadow lark,
    As she flits and flutters,
    And laughs at the thunder when it mutters.
    O happy bird, of heart most gay
    To sing when skies are gray!

When the clouds are full,
  And the tempest master
    Lets the loud winds sweep
    From his bosom deep
Like heralds of some dire disaster,
    Then the heart, alone,
    To itself makes moan;
And the songs come slow,
    While the tears fall fleeter,
    And silence than song by far seems sweeter.
    Oh, few are they along the way
    Who sing when skies are gray!

The Seedling.

As a quiet little seedling
  Lay within its darksome bed,
To itself it fell a talking,
  And this is what it said:

"I am not so very robust,
  But I'll do the best I can";
And the seedling from that moment
  Its work of life began.

So it pushed a little leaflet
  Up into the light of day,
To examine the surroundings
  And show the rest the' way.

The leaflet liked the prospect,
  So it called its brother, Stem;
Then two other leaflets heard it,
  And quickly followed them.

To be sure, the haste and hurry
  Made the seedling sweat and pant;
But almost before it knew it
  It found itself a plant.

The sunshine poured upon it,
  And the clouds they gave a shower;
And the little plant kept growing
  Till it found itself a flower.

Little folks, be like the seedling,
  Always do the best you can;
Every child must share life's labor
  Just as well as every man.

And the sun and showers will help you
  Through the lonesome, struggling hours,
Till you raise to light and beauty
  Virtue's fair, unfading flowers.

Poor Withered Rose.

A SONG.

Poor withered rose, she gave it me,
Half in revenge and half in glee;
Its petals not so pink by half
As are her lips when curled to laugh,
As are her cheeks when dimples gay
In merry mischief o'er them play.

CHORUS.

  Forgive, forgive, it seems unkind
  To cast thy petals to the wind;
  But it is right, and lest I err
  So scatter I all thoughts of her.

Poor withered rose, so like my heart,
That wilts at sorrow's cruel dart.
Who hath not felt the winter's blight
When every hope seemed warm and bright?
Who doth not know love unreturned,
E'en when the heart most wildly burned?

Poor withered rose, thou liest dead;
Too soon thy beauty's bloom hath fled.
'Tis not without a tearful ruth
I watch decay thy blushing youth;
And though thy life goes out in dole,
Thy perfume lingers in my soul.

Confirmation.

He was a poet who wrote clever verses,
 . And folks said he had fine poetical taste;
But his father, a practical farmer, accused him
 Of letting the strength of his arm go to waste.

He called on his sweetheart each Saturday evening,
 As pretty a maiden as man ever faced,
And there he confirmed the old man's accusation
 By letting the strength of his arm go to *waist.*

Nora: A Serenade.

Ah, Nora, my Nora, the light fades away,
 While Night like a spirit steals up o'er the hills;
The thrush from his tree where he chanted all day,
 No longer his music in ecstasy trills.
Then, Nora, be near me; thy presence doth cheer me,
 Thine eye hath a gleam that is truer than gold.
I cannot but love thee; so do not reprove me,
 If the strength of my passion should make me too bold.

CHORUS.

 Nora, pride of my heart,—
 Rosy cheeks, cherry lips, sparkling with glee,—
 Wake from thy slumbers, wherever thou art;
 Wake from thy slumbers to me.

Ah, Nora, my Nora, there's love in the air,—
 It stirs in the numbers that thrill in my brain;
Oh, sweet, sweet is love with its mingling of care,
 Though joy travels only a step before pain.
Be roused from thy slumbers and list to my numbers;
 My heart is poured out in this song unto thee.
Oh, be thou not cruel, thou treasure, thou jewel;
 Turn thine ear to my pleading and hearken to me.

Evening.

The moon begins her stately ride
  Across the summer sky;
The happy wavelets lash the shore,—
  The tide is rising high.

Beneath some friendly blade of grass
  The lazy beetle cowers;
The coffers of the air are filled
  With offerings from the flowers.

And slowly buzzing o'er my head
  A swallow wings her flight;
I hear the weary plowman sing
  As falls the restful night.

To Pfrimmer.

LINES ON READING "DRIFTWOOD."

Driftwood gathered here and there
Along the beach of time;
Now and then a chip of truth
'Mid boards and boughs of rhyme;
Driftwood gathered day by day,—
The cypress and the oak,—
Twigs that in some former time
From sturdy home trees broke.
Did this wood come floating thick
All along down "Injin Crik"?
Or did kind tides bring it thee
From the past's receding sea
Down the stream of memory?

Sympathy.

The tear another's tears bring forth,
   The sigh which answers sigh,
The pulse that beats at other's woes,
   E'en though our own be nigh,

A balm to bathe the wounded heart
   Where sorrow's hand hath lain,
The link divine from soul to soul
   That makes us one in pain,—

Sweet sympathy, benignant ray,
   Light of the soul doth shine;
In it is human nature giv'n
   A touch of the divine.

My Love Irene.

Farewell, farewell, my love Irene;
   The pangs of sadness stir my breast;
Though many miles may intervene,
   My soul's with thine, in East or West.
Go where thou wilt, to wealth or fame;
Win for thyself or praise or blame,—
My love shall ever be the same,
     My love Irene.

Farewell, farewell, my love Irene;
   Oh, sad decree, that we must part!
The wound is deep, the pain is keen
   That agitates mine aching heart.
My feverish eyes burn up their tears,
I cannot still my doubts and fears;
And this one sigh the night wind hears,—
     My love Irene.

Farewell, farewell, my love Irene;
  The morning's gray now floods the sky;
The sun peeps from his misty screen;
  Mine only love, good-bye, good-bye.
All love must fade, all life must die,
The smile must turn into the sigh.
Alas! how hard to say good-bye,
    My love Irene.

Common Things.

I like to hear of wealth and gold,
  And El Doradoes in their glory;
I like for silks and satins bold
  To sweep and rustle through a story.

The nightingale is sweet of song;
  The rare exotic smells divinely;
And knightly men who stride along,
  The role heroic carry finely.

But then, upon the other hand,
  Our minds have got a way of running
To things that aren't quite so grand,
  Which, maybe, we were best in shunning.

For some of us still like to see
  The poor man in his dwelling narrow,
The hollyhock, the bumblebee,
  The meadow lark, and chirping sparrow.

We like the man who soars and sings
  With high and lofty inspiration;
But he who sings of common things
  Shall always share our admiration.

Goin' Back.

He stood beside the station rail,
A negro aged and bent and frail.
His palsied hands like the aspen shook,
And a mute appeal was in his look;
His every move was pained and slow,
And his matted hair was white as snow.
He noted our questioning looks, and said,
With a solemn shake of his hoary head:
"I reckon you're wonderin', an' well you may,
Whar an ol' man lak me's a goin' to-day.
I've lived in this town fur thirty years,
An' known alike my joys an' tears,
An' I've labored hard year out, year in;
But now I'm a goin' back agin
To the blue grass medders an' fiel's o' co'n
In the dear ol' State whar I was bo'n.
It's the same ol' tale that I have to tell,—
An' thar's few o' my race but knows it well,—
When fust the proclamation come
I felt too free to stay at home.
Freedom, it seemed, was a gift divine,
An' I thought the whole wide world was mine
Then I was spry, an' my hair was black,
An' this troublesome crook wasn't in my back;
My soul was allus full o' song,
Fur my heart was light, an' my limbs was strong,
An' I wasn't afeared to show my face
To the sturdiest worker on the place.
Well, I caught the fever that ruled the day,
An', finally, northward made my way.
They said that things were better North,
An' a man was held at his honest worth.
Well, it may be so, but I have some doubt,
An' thirty years ain't wiped it out.

Thar was lots of things in the North to admire,
Though they hadn't the warmth an' passion an' fire
That all my life I'd been ust to seein'
An' thought belonged to a human bein'.
An' a thing I could'nt help but miss
Was the real ol' Southern heartiness.
But year after year I worried along,
While deep in my heart the yearnin' strong
Grew stronger an' fiercer to visit once more
The well loved scenes o' my native shore.
But money was skeerce, an' time went on,
Till now full thirty years have gone
Ere I turn my aged steps to roam
Back to my ol' Kaintucky home,
Back to the ol' Kaintucky sights,
Back to the scene o' my youth's delights,
Back whar my heart was full o' glee,
Back whar I fust found liberty.
E'en now as I think the ol' times o'er,
An' o' the joy they held in store,—
Yes, even now, on life's dark side,
My heart swells out with honest pride.
Oh, praise the Lamb, that I shall see
Once more the land so dear to me.
Don't mind an ol' man's tears, but say
It's joy, he's goin' back to-day."

Justice.

Enthroned upon the mighty truth,
    Within the confines of the laws,
True Justice seeth not the man,
    But only hears his cause.

Unconscious of his creed or race,
She cannot see, but only weighs;
For Justice with unbandaged eyes
Would be oppression in disguise.

Night of Love.

The moon has left the sky, love,
    The stars are hiding now,
And frowning on the world, love,
    Night bares her sable brow.
The snow is on the ground, love,
    And cold and keen the air is.
I'm singing here to you, love;
    You're dreaming there in Paris.

But this is Nature's law, love,
    Though just it may not seem,
That men should wake to sing, love,
    While maidens sleep and dream.
Them care may not molest, love,
    Nor stir them from their slumbers,
Though midnight find the swain, love,
    Still halting o'er his numbers.

I watch the rosy dawn, love,
    Come stealing up the east,
While all things round rejoice, love,
    That Night her reign has ceased.
The lark will soon be heard, love,
    And on his way be winging;
When Nature's poets wake, love,
    Why should a man be singing?

INDEX.

61